SALT and LIGHT
POCKET GUIDES

COMING TO GRIPS WITH UNANSWERED PRAYER

COMING TO GRIPS WITH UNANSWERED PRAYER

ERWIN W. LUTZER

MOODY PRESS

CHICAGO

ISBN: 0-8024-3543-2

1 2 3 4 5 6 Printing/VP/Year 94 93 92 91 90

Printed in the United States of America

Coming to Grips with
Unanswered Prayer

" Since God didn't answer all those prayers, I'm not going to bother Him with another request again. What's the use? I don't want to be hurt one more time!" The woman was bitter, and whether justified or not, her attitude was certainly understandable.

Her young pastor had been diagnosed with cancer. His congregation took their responsibility to pray for him seriously. They signed up for round-the-clock prayer so that at least one person was praying for him twenty-four hours a day. Additional prayer meetings were scheduled. The deacons anointed him with oil and prayed. Some fasted and prayed for days on end, beseeching God to heal him.

When he went into the hospital for treatment, some believers came to him with the assurance that he would be healed. God had shown them that this miracle was His will, they said, and He had confirmed it by giving the same assurance to several people independently.

Even when he collapsed into a coma, his wife and small children were assured that this sickness was not unto death. Though God would allow him to come unto the jaws of death, he would be delivered in the end.

But that was not to be.

He died, with his friends and family still full of faith that God would intervene and restore him to health. But unlike Lazarus, there was no earthly resurrection for this man.

Perhaps you can understand the disillusionment and even betrayal these church members felt. Over in the nursing home lived older people who had long since lost touch with reality. They no longer recognized their children; they longed for death, but it eluded them. Yet God took a young man with a life of fruitful ministry ahead of him, leaving behind a grieving young family and a sorrowing church.

If God doesn't answer the concerted prayers of His people offered in the name of Christ and for His glory, why bother with prayer? Should we assume that prayer does not affect God?

When such prayers go unanswered, the easy response is to blame it on sin in the lives of the intercessors or on unbelief. Granted, there is no question that sin is a hindrance to prayer. David admitted, "If I regard wickedness in my heart, the Lord will not hear" (Psalm 66:18). But in the case of the pastor described above, that answer is too simplistic. He was a godly man who regularly asked God to search his heart to reveal any sin that needed to be confessed. Doubtless the congregation had its share of carnality, but no overt sin had gone unconfessed or unpunished. Hundreds who prayed for this man were Spirit-filled Christians who sought God for direction in their prayers.

What about unbelief? Christ could do no miracles in Caperneum because of the city's unbelief. Could that be the reason God did not answer the many prayers for that pastor? Perhaps, but it is unlikely. People actually believed—firmly believed—that he would be healed. God had given them this assurance, or so they thought. Far from being filled with unbelief, some of that young pastor's friends actually seemed to believe too much.

James wrote, "You ask and do not receive, because you ask with wrong motives, so that you may spend it on your pleasures" (4:3). Though in some cases self-interest is certainly a hindrance to prayer, those who prayed for this man knew that his healing would contribute to the glory of God. They yearned that the medical doctors be proved wrong in their pessimistic prognosis. What a witness his healing would have been to unbelievers, as well as to skeptical believers!

Where did the will of God fit into this scenario? John wrote, "And this is the confidence which we have before Him, that, if we ask anything according to His will, He hears us. And if we know that He hears us in whatever we ask, we know that we have the requests which we have asked from Him" (1 John 5:14-15). So the question arises, how do we know what the will of God is? In retrospect, it seems obvious that it was God's will for that pastor to die. But how could the congregation have known that? In praying for his restoration were they actually praying contrary to the will of God?

We must tread carefully here, for the phrase "the will of God" is used in two different senses in Scripture. Sometimes it refers to the decree of God, by which God runs everything in His universe. Paul says God "works all things after the counsel of

His will" (Ephesians 1:11). In this general sense, virtually everything, even evil, is either directly or indirectly God's will.

The more popular use of the expression "the will of God" refers to the desires God has revealed regarding our conduct and choices in life. For example, Paul wrote, "In everything give thanks; for this is God's will for you in Christ Jesus" (1 Thessalonians 5:18). Or again, "So then do not be foolish, but understand what the will of the Lord is" (Ephesians 5:17).

When we speak of unanswered prayer we wrestle with this second understanding of the will of God. What we want to know is: what was God's plan for that pastor's life? Was it really God's desire for him to die, or was his death the result of spiritual negligence on his part? Was it because of the congregation's unbelief?

In my experience as a pastor I have come to believe that unanswered prayer is one of the most common stumbling blocks to spiritual growth. We've all begged and pleaded about situations that we know God could easily change; we have enlisted the prayer support of others and believed. But many times the heavens have remained silent. So the logical conclusion appears to be that God does not care.

God seems to tease us with promises that are too good to be true. And when we act on them, He does not always come through for us exactly as we think a loving, dependable God should. Thus our hopes, which are held aloft by His promises, are dashed to the ground by His apparently cruel indifference.

Philip Yancey quotes Barbara Sanderville, a young paraplegic, who put it vividly:

> Knowing that God had the power to heal me but wouldn't . . . made me very bitter. I would read Isaiah 53, and 1 Peter 2:24, and accuse God of holding the promise of healing before me like a piece of meat before a starving dog. He tempted me by showing me the potential but never quite allowing me to reach it.[1]

Who can calculate the hurt that overwhelms those who have prayed for a wayward child, only to learn that he has died in a tragic accident or by drug overdose? Who can measure the pain of those who have besought God for healing or the companionship of a marriage partner or harmony in their home? Yet these and a thousand other requests so often go unanswered.

Some Christians are so disappointed with God that they don't even want to get close to Him anymore. They stay at a safe distance, fearing that their confidence will be shattered again.

I'm convinced that the presence of unconfessed sin in our lives, unbelief, and selfish motives all hinder prayer. But the absence of these factors does not guarantee that prayer will be answered. You and I have seen godly people pray with the purest of motives, yet their requests lay like unopened envelopes upon a celestial table.

I've heard it said that God answers all prayers—He just answers some by saying no. That's not exactly comforting. A child would not likely say to his friends, "My father answers all my requests—he just said no when I asked him for a dollar."

In an attempt to find satisfying answers to these questions, we need to discuss the will of God, the sovereignty of God, and faith. But for now, let us survey some of the unanswered prayers in the Bible to see if we can uncover clues that explain how God responds to His people. Later, we will try to find the hidden purposes that God might have in letting our prayers go unanswered.

There are three different kinds of unanswered prayers. In some cases the answer is *delayed*. At other times it is *disguised*, that is, God answers the prayer but in an entirely different way than we had expected. Sometimes the answer is *denied;* the door is shut, and the answer is no. We can learn from each of these responses.

THE ANSWER DELAYED

Often God chooses to answer our prayers but does so according to His own schedule. One day Abraham cried out to God in confusion. Twenty-five years earlier, the Lord had promised that he would be the father of a great nation. But, of course, to see that promise fulfilled, he had to have a child.

So Abraham sought the Lord: "O Lord God, what wilt Thou give me, since I am childless, and the heir of my house is Eliezer of Damascus?" (Genesis 15:2). God had already specified that the child would come from Abraham's own body, but he was wondering whether he had heard correctly. Sarah was barren, and he himself was approaching old age. Perhaps his heir would come through his servant.

Abraham did not have to wrestle with the question of whether God wanted him to have posterity. Since he had had direct communication with God, he did not have to rely on subjective assurance, an inner voice, or inexplicable peace. The will of God was perfectly clear.

Yet despite the clarity of the promise, Abraham began to doubt God and actually tried to force an answer to his own prayer. Specifically (at the suggestion of Sarah), he had sexual relations with the Egyptian maid Hagar, and Ishmael was born.

That practice was common in Abraham's day, but it did not excuse the fact that he doubted God and chose to sin in order to get an answer to God's promise. If only he had waited. Eventually, God was going to perform a miracle in Sarah's body and in his own, as well. Isaac was the fulfillment of the promise.

Abraham confused the *delay* of God with the *denial* of God. Sometimes we give up too easily; sometimes we are too quick to consign our lot to fate. But God answers us according to His schedule.

All who walk with God must learn to wait for answers to their prayers, even in instances in which the will of God has been clearly revealed. For example, Paul was given a promise that he would carry the gospel to Rome (Acts 23:11). Yet he was imprisoned in Caesarea for two full years before that came about. During that time he probably wondered why God was being so slow to fulfill His will.

But God uses delays. He knew that Paul needed a rest, and He used that time in Caesarea to renew Paul physically for the trek to Rome. What is more, Paul had the opportunity to put his own advice into practice. He had always taught the value of patience (which is really endurance), and in Caesarea he had a chance to deepen his own inner life. "Tribulation," he wrote, "brings about perseverance" (Romans 5:3).

Someone has said that *the work God does within us while we wait is probably as important as the thing we are waiting for.*

The delays of unanswered prayer give us two opportunities:

1. Patience and faith are developed. These virtues are precious to God.

2. Worship of God is increased as we come to appreciate His timing. It has been observed that we get the chicken by hatching the egg, not by snatching it. Sometimes we must patiently wait as we watch God's schedule unfold. At times when we say, "God said no," we really mean that He said, "Not now."

THE ANSWER DISGUISED

Sometimes God answers our prayers—but not the way we expect Him to. One day God confided to

Abraham that the cities of Sodom and Gomorrah would be destroyed because of a heavy concentration of wickedness in the area. Abraham was devastated, for his nephew Lot lived in Sodom with his wife and children. God's statement sparked an emotional time of intercession, as Abraham pleaded with God to spare the city if some righteous could be found in it. When that time was over, the agreement was that if as few as ten righteous were found, God would not destroy the city (Genesis 18:22-33). Abraham left, confident that the city would not be destroyed.

The next day Abraham went out to look at the valley and saw billows of smoke ascending toward heaven. God was raining fire and brimstone upon the city. He realized that he had miscalculated—evidently there were not even ten righteous in the city after all.

As it turned out, there were only *four* righteous: Lot and his wife and their daughters. If God had destroyed the city with them in it, He would not have been breaking faith with Abraham. And God *did* destroy the city. Yet God also gave Abraham what he wanted. The patriarch was deeply burdened for his nephew Lot and his family. What Abraham did not foresee was that God would take the righteous out before He destroyed the cities.

Notice this divine commentary, "Thus it came about, when God destroyed the cities of the valley, that God remembered Abraham, and sent Lot out of the midst of the overthrow" (Genesis 19:29). God remembered Abraham! In the end, the patriarch got what he wanted but not what he had expected.

David also prayed about a deep desire that God had put into his heart. His dream was to build a temple for God in Jerusalem. Was that a good desire? Yes. The desire would have passed any test we might wish to put to it. For one thing, it was a task that God wanted done. Jerusalem was the city God had chosen to be the spiritual capital for His people. It was God's will to have a temple built there.

Second, David had the time and the ability to do it. It fell within the range of his aptitudes and "giftedness."

Third, his desire was confirmed by a prophet of God, Nathan. David told Nathan about his vision, and Nathan responded, "Do all that is in your heart, for God is with you" (1 Chronicles 17:2).

Fourth, and most important, David had a pure motive. He did not want to build a monument to himself but to God. Indeed, the Lord said he did well that the desire was in his heart (2 Chronicles 6:8).

Yet later, God spoke to the prophet Nathan and told him that the answer to David's desire was no. David would not be the one to build the Temple because he was a man of bloodshed.

God said no to David with great tenderness and encouragement. David was given some new promises. His would be a great name. What's more, rather than David's building a house for God, God promised to build a house for David. The Lord would give him posterity (a house) and a throne that will last forever (the details are in 1 Chronicles 17). Thus David got to build a house after all but not the kind he had expected. The house he built for God was the family line through which Christ later came.

But there is still more to the story. God promised that the house (Temple) that David had prayed about would would be built by David's son Solomon, whose mother was Bathsheba. And David had a part in that project—he gathered materials for the building. David put stonecutters to work, gathered large quantities of iron and brass, and purchased timbers and cedar logs (1 Chronicles 22:1-4).

What lessons can we learn from prayers that have disguised answers —prayers that are answered, but not in the way we expect?

1. *When God says no, He may substitute something else to take the place of your desire.* If your desire to go to the mission field is unfulfilled, He may enable you to send someone else. If you cannot have children, you may be able to adopt a child. If you want a marriage partner, that desire to love someone may have to be funneled into the lives of other people. All of us at some time or another will have to live with unfulfilled desires, but God is able to give us the grace to endure—if we understand that our desires will probably be redirected.

Let me put it this way. Suppose you have two desires. If the stronger of the two is fulfilled, then the unfulfillment of the lesser one becomes tolerable. George Mueller said that the chief duty of every Christian is to "have his soul happy in God." If that desire is met in our intimacy with the Almighty, then the other struggles of life become manageable.

2. *We must have the grace to see that God's substitute answer is better than our original request.* David worshiped God after He said no to the desire of David's heart. He was able to recognize the goodness and kindness of God, in spite of his disappoint-

ment. First, the Temple would be built. And, incredibly, it would be built by David's son who had been born to Bathsheba, the woman whom David had wronged—the woman whose husband David had killed. Out of the mess that David had made, God promised to do something beautiful and lasting.

Second, David was permitted to have a part in the building of the Temple. Through gathering materials and giving advice, David played a vital role in the project. His dream was realized through someone else, but *it did come to pass.*

Finally, David built a house, a lineage that would produce the Christ and the eventual establishment of His kingdom forever. David's prayer was not answered according to his specifications, but I believe his desire was fulfilled.

Sometimes when God says no, He may be pointing us in a different direction. In such cases we may get nothing that we asked for, yet all that we hoped for.

> I asked for strength that I might
>   do great things;
> He gave me infirmity that I
>   might do better things.
> I asked for riches that I might be
>   happy;

He gave me poverty that I might
   be wise.
I asked for power that I might
   sway men;
He gave me weakness that I
   might learn God's grace.
I asked for companionship that I
   might be fulfilled;
He gave me loneliness that I
   might feel my need of God.
I received nothing I asked for
   but all that I hoped for.

God's no is often an invitation to a yes we had not thought of before. Look for the answer in unexpected places. It may simply be disguised.

THE ANSWER DENIED

The apostle Paul was given many special revelations and was even caught up to the third heaven, that is, to the abode of God, to hear and see things he was not permitted to tell others.

To keep him humble, he was given a "thorn in the flesh" that was a constant reminder of his weakness (2 Corinthians 12:7-10). What was the thorn? The Greek word is *skolops*, which means "a stake," such as was used when prisoners were impaled (the ancient practice was to inflict as much pain as possible). Perhaps Paul suffered from malaria, which one commentator says was as painful as "a red-hot bar thrust through the forehead." Whatever the thorn, it was persistent and painful.

Where did the thorn come from? The *immediate* cause was "a messenger of Satan" (v. 7). The devil was the one who caused Paul's thorn, for he has always delighted in inflicting suffering.

But God was the *ultimate* cause of the trial. "There was given me a thorn in the flesh" (v. 7). And when he asked that it be taken away, Paul did not appeal to Satan but to God. "I entreated the Lord three times" (v. 8). The thorn was from God, but Satan's messenger was permitted to work under God's watchful supervision.

Paul's cry was specific. He wanted the obstruction taken out of the way. It was also persistent. He besought the Lord three times, undeterred by God's apparent reluctance. He met the requirement of prevailing, believing prayer.

The first two times, God didn't say anything. But after the third prayer, God spoke to shed light on Paul's dilemma. The reply: *request not granted*. Paul's prayer did not budge the thorn; God decreed that it would stay put.

However, that was not the end of the story. God did not stand idly by, watching Paul struggle. God gave him something he hadn't asked for —something that enabled him to accept the negative answer.

Paul received two gifts:

The first was grace. He received heavenly strength for the need of the moment. A river flowed from the heart of God and flooded Paul's soul. We usually think of grace as God's unmerited favor bestowed at the time of salvation, and that is true. But grace is also a gift given at the time of special need: "He giveth more grace."

Second, he received strength in the midst of his weakness. The infirmity remained, but there was divine enablement. He was given the power needed to counteract the pain.

How did Paul view being turned down by the Almighty? Suddenly he regarded the pain differently. Rather than seeing it as a hindrance to his ministry, he began to see it as a plus. "Therefore, I will rather boast about my weaknesses," he said.

Pain was no longer his enemy, and now he could say, "My enemy is working for my good." The thorn became a blessing. "Most gladly, therefore, I will rather boast about my weaknesses, that the power of Christ may dwell in me" (v. 9).

From that unanswered prayer, strength emerged. Paul became a better man, a more effective witness.

The thorn grew into a rose; the pain became power. Satan could not stop Paul; the apostle was strengthened instead.

Here are some lessons to learn when our request is denied.

1. *God does not lay a burden upon us that is too heavy for us to bear.* If you were carrying a bag of cement, there would be two ways to make it lighter: either someone could help you lift it, or you could be given stronger arms and legs to carry it. Sometimes God chooses the first response, sometimes the second. Either way the burden is made bearable. Paul learned that it didn't matter how heavy his burden was as long as God gave him the ability to bear it.

2. *The thorns of life are specially chosen for those to whom they are given.* Paul said, "There was given to me a thorn in the flesh."

When I buy a suit, it is generally from the rack in the store. Only once, when I was in Hong Kong, did I have a suit tailor-made. I was measured and remeasured to make sure that the measurements were accurate. It fit perfectly.

All of God's trials are made to order; none are given indiscriminately. To ask why He gives a specific trial to one and no trial to another is meaningless. God always has a purpose in trials. The thorns that won't budge are for our good.

It is pointless to suggest, as some have, that if the apostle Paul had confessed the pride in his life, the thorn would have been removed. It is interesting that he does not say he had actually become proud. Rather, the thorn was preventative, that is, its purpose was to keep him from self-exaltation in the future. If we think that means that God spanks us for something we haven't done yet, we miss the fact that God, who knows all things, has a right to discipline us, either because we have already sinned or because we are about to sin. All that we can expect is grace to bear the trial.

When paraplegic Joni Eareckson Tada was asked how how she can bear her handicap, she replied:

> I feel that he will never give us a burden we cannot bear. You know, I look at some of my friends who are more disabled than I, and say, *I couldn't handle it.* I have a friend, Vicki, who at best can only move her head from side to side. I at least can flail my arms and shrug my shoulders. She's far more disabled than I. I've said to her, "Vicki, I don't know how you do it," and she says, "Well, with God's grace I can." When Vicki

24

looks at some of her friends who are hooked up to breathing machines, she doesn't know how they do it. All of us are placed somewhere on this scale of suffering. Some of us suffer more than others, but wherever God places you and me on the scale, he gives us accompanying grace to handle it.[2]

God weighs out our thorns with the same care that a pharmacist weighs out prescription medicine. His grace is sufficient to those who submit to His Word.

3. *Satanic conflict serves to strengthen us, not hinder us.* If we followed the popular teaching of today, we would assume that Paul should have been able to simply rebuke the influence of Satan in his life and be freed from his infirmity. However, that would not have worked for the simple reason that *God wanted Paul to endure the thorn.*

Please do not assume that we should stoically accept the activity of Satan in the life of a believer. I strongly believe that Christians tolerate far too much harassment from the powers of darkness. God wants us to route the enemy and subdue him. Whenever Satan comes to tempt us or to disrupt our emotional lives, we must insist that he flee. Paul's situation was unique in that it involved only a physical infirmity, a trial of the body, not the defeat of the soul. Also, he had specific revelation from God as to its purpose.

Yet from Paul we learn that when the request is denied, God gives us grace to accept the answer. We have the assurance that God can use our disappointment for His glory and honor.

SOME HARD QUESTIONS

All of this is of some help in understanding the mystery of unanswered prayer, but some tough questions remain.

To us, God often seems to be hard-hearted or indifferent to the plight of His children. A mother nervously attends her sick child, but he eventually dies an excruciating death from leukemia. Worse, children cry to God for deliverance from abuse, yet God does not answer their prayers. We wonder, does He listen? Does He care?

Dorie Van Stone in her book *No Place to Cry* (Moody, 1990), tells how she was sexually abused in foster homes when she was growing up. She became a Christian at the age of thirteen and knew God's presence. But during those dark days of physical and sexual abuse, her prayers for protection often went unanswered. Why didn't God deliver her from her tormentors? Such stories cause us to wonder whether God really cares or not. To the casual observer, He appears to be cruel.

Contrast that image with that of an earthly father who loves his child. He would never allow him to die a painful, untimely death from cancer if it were in his power to prevent it. He would never stand by and watch his child being tortured year after year; instead, he would swiftly intervene and actively seek justice. We are told that our heavenly Father loves us more than our earthly father does. Why the difference in their reactions to our needs?

These questions must now be addressed in light of a biblical understanding of the relationship God has with His people.

THE PROMISES OF GOD

Effective prayer means that we "claim the promises." Often we hear people say, "God gave me this promise." Such a claim may be quite true, but strictly speaking the same promises are given to everyone. Since the Bible is for all of God's people, it is misleading to imply that some receive a promise that might be denied to others.

Unfortunately, some promises are misapplied.

Some teach that the Scriptures tell us it is God's will to heal everyone who is sick. Basing their claims on certain texts, they assure us that physical healing is the explicit will of God for every believer who meets the requirements of holiness and faith.

The best-known promises on this subject are found in Isaiah 53 and are quoted again in the New Testament. In Matthew 8:17 we read that Christ went about healing people "in order that what was spoken through Isaiah the prophet might be fulfilled, saying, 'He Himself took our infirmities, and carried away our diseases.'"

Peter wrote, "He Himself bore our sins in His body on the cross, that we might die to sin and live to righteousness; for by His wounds you were healed" (1 Peter 2:24).

Some theologians who are skeptical of divine healing have labored to prove that the healing spoken of in these passages is spiritual, not physical. But the context in Matthew and the implication in Peter is that Christ did indeed die for our physical bodies. In fact, it is consistent with Scripture to affirm that Christ came to redeem the whole man—body, soul, and spirit.

But does this mean that we can have physical healing whenever we prayerfully meet certain conditions? Clearly, the answer is no. Although Christ died for our bodies as well as for our souls, we will not see the fulfillment of that aspect of redemption until we are resurrected into glory. Christ came to redeem us from sin, yet we still have a sin nature; He came to destroy death, yet we die; He came to redeem our bodies, yet we are subject to accidents, poisons, and the frailty of the flesh.

Many who teach that divine healing is instantly available wear glasses, get arthritis, and have implanted hearing aids. All these infirmities bear eloquent testimony to the fact that in this life we see only the beginning of redemption. Yes, sometimes God does heal (particularly as seen in the ministry of Christ), but even then the healing is merely a postponement of future illness and death. None of the healing Christ did on earth was permanent. Every one of those He restored eventually became sick again and died.

This misunderstanding of the promises of Scripture has been the cause of much grief in the Christian community. People who claim healing, insisting that God is obligated to keep His promises, often end up feeling betrayed. When healing does not occur, they point to these verses of Scripture and say that God cannot be trusted. Or, they try to find some other reason—unbelief, unconfessed sin, and so on—to explain why they were not healed, in a vain effort to protect God's reputation.

Others point to the promise of James that the sick should call for the elders of the church, and, if the sick one is anointed with oil, "the prayer offered in faith will restore the one who is sick, and the Lord will raise him up, and if he has committed sins, they will be forgiven him" (5:15). That cannot mean that a believer will always be raised up; if it did, logic would require that a person could always escape death. He could call the elders of the church each time he became ill and be healed repeatedly.

The answer to this prayer is actually dependent on "the prayer of faith," which means that in specific instances God may grant the elders the united faith to believe in the restoration of the individual. In other instances they may not have such faith. The "raising up" takes place only when God grants the gift of faith for that particular situation. It is impossible for us to manufacture such faith on our own.

Other promises related to prayer come to mind. Christ said to His disciples, "And whatever you ask in My name, that will I do, that the Father may be glorified in the Son. If you ask Me anything in My name, I will do it" (John 14:13-14). If we interpret that statement to be a carte blanche affirmation that we will always get whatever we want, we will be disappointed. We have already documented enough cases of unanswered prayer to know that we often do not receive what we ask for.

Some have suggested that that promise applied only to the apostles and not to their followers. It is interesting that the apostle Paul, who wrote most of the letters of the New Testament, which are for this church era, does not make any such promise about prayer. Rather, he exhorts us, "Be anxious for nothing, but in everything by prayer and supplication with thanksgiving, let your requests be made known to God. And the peace of God, which surpasses all comprehension, shall guard your hearts and your minds in Christ Jesus" (Philippians 4:6-7). He gives no assurance that our requests will be fulfilled—only that we will have the peace of Christ and the ability to accept whatever God gives us.

Of course, even if we claim Christ's promise for ourselves, it has certain limitations to it. First, He says that whatever we ask "in His name" we will receive. That means that the request must be consistent

31

with the character of Christ. As an ambassador speaks in the name of the king, so we must be subject to the will and purposes of Christ. He does not lend His good name to just anyone. Some take it upon themselves, of course, and even do miracles "in His name," yet they are barred from the kingdom of heaven (Matthew 7:22-23).

Second, we are to ask "that the Father might be glorified in the Son." Our prayers must be free of self-interest and must instead seek the glory and approval of God. The main purpose of prayer is not to get us out of bankruptcy or lessen the pain of an inflamed tumor, though the Almighty is concerned with such matters. The primary motive of prayer should be the glory of God and the vindication of His honor.

The example of Christ is instructive here. We know that He lived for the glory of God. He pleased the Father, who was glorified at the Son's expense.

Christ's entire life was bathed in prayer, and He prayed no prayer that was not fully answered. The closest He ever came to using prayer as a means to escape physical and spiritual distress was when He prayed in Gethsemane: "Abba! Father! All things are possible for Thee; remove this cup from Me; yet not what I will, but what Thou wilt" (Mark 14:26).

Christ had every right to ask the Father for anything; why did He not insist that He be exempted from the impending torture of the cross? The answer is that *it was God's will that Christ suffer.* The prayer of Gethsemane was the means that Christ used to receive the grace and power to do the will of God. Prayer enabled Christ to gather strength to go through with His assignment; it was not the means of delivering Him from it.

The bottom line is that promises such as the one in John 14:13-14 must always be subjected to the overriding will of God—a will that may involve pain, injustice, and death, just as it did for our Savior.

This naturally leads us to the question posed at the beginning of this booklet: if the will of God for us involves an untimely death (as in the case of the young pastor), how are we to know this? How can we pray effectively if we don't know what the will of God is in a specific situation?

THE WILL OF GOD

Perhaps the best way for us to understand how to pray according to the will of God is to examine Christ's prayers for His disciples and the apostle Paul's prayers for his fellow believers. What is so surprising in these prayers is the absence of any reference to wealth, health, or personal comforts—the very subjects that occupy so much space on our own personal prayer lists. The fact that Christ and the apostles concentrated primarily on the spiritual welfare of individuals rather than on their health, comfort, or financial needs is evident in Christ's promises to His disciples in the Upper Room and in prayers such as are recorded in Luke 22:31-32 and John 17:1-26.

The apostle Paul stressed the spiritual welfare of believers almost exclusively in his prayers (Ephesians 1:18-23; 3:14-21; Philippians 1:9-11; Colossians 1:9-12). Space forbids a detailed analysis of these prayers, so I encourage you to read them on your own. The themes are: faithfulness, the defeat of Satan, spiritual perception, fruitfulness, and an increased desire to know and serve God. The emphasis is on the need for grace to successfully endure hardship rather than on means to escape it.

In other words, when a person is ill or has financial problems or is treated unjustly, we have no biblical basis to know what the will of God is. A young woman asks, "How do I know it is God's will that I have a marriage partner?" A parent hovering over the bed of a sick child asks, "How do I know whether it is the will of God that my child be healed?" In these and many other instances we must humbly confess that we do not know what the will of God is, for He has not seen fit to reveal it.

What we do know is that it is the will of God for *Christ to be victorious within us, whether the circumstances change or not.* A Christlike response to the injustices and tragedies of life is always God's will.

Does that mean that we should not pray about those matters about which we are in doubt? Of course not! Christ prayed in Gethsemane, though it did not prevent His going to the cross; Paul prayed that his thorn be removed, though prayer did not remove it. We should pray about everything, letting our requests be made known unto God, and the peace of God will keep our hearts and minds in Christ Jesus (Philippians 4:6-7). As we shall see in a moment, prayer has many benefits, even if the requests go unanswered. We make our requests to God and then commit everything into His hands.

What about those who claim to have special knowledge of the will of God that is not revealed in the Scriptures? Many people affirm that the Lord has shown them His specific will about particular situations. Thus in the absence of a scriptural promise they appeal to "inner peace," a subjective voice, or a sense of assurance.

But it is often difficult for us to distinguish our desires from the will of God. We so earnestly want to see our prayer answered—after all, it seems so reasonable—that we identify the desire itself with the will of God. It may be His will—but not necessarily.

Second, we think we can confirm our desire by the degree of peace God gives us about the situation. The more peace we have, the more confident we are that God is going to answer according to our desires.

That may explain why so many people in the example above believed that their pastor would be healed. They misread the will of God but not because they lacked holiness, sincerity, or even faith. The reason is that they *mistook the peace of God for the plan of God.* God granted them peace about the situation, and they took that as a sign that God would answer as requested. It is easy for any one of us to make that mistake. We pray about a matter and give it wholly to God. The Lord graciously floods our souls with peace, and we interpret that to mean that our prayer will be answered according to our specifications.

At times it may be possible to ascertain the will of God subjectively.

But even those who claim they can do so often admit that their perceptions and impressions have been wrong. *In many matters we simply do not know what the will of God is.* When those matters are left wholly to Him, we can rejoice in peace that His will, though presently unknown to us, will be done.

The closer we walk with God, the more we may be able to discern His will in those unrevealed matters. His desires can more often become ours. He may give us burdens that are in accord with the plan He intends to accomplish. But in the absence of specific biblical promises, we simply cannot confirm the specific will of God in each situation.

THE SOVEREIGN PURPOSE OF GOD

Having come this far, we must now ask, Why is God's will so obscure? Shouldn't the will of God be straightforward and reasonable? What could be plainer than the fact that it is His will to heal a young pastor? If it isn't His will, it should be!

The Bible is filled with examples of God's sovereign dealings that prove without question that His ways are not our ways and that His hidden purposes are not revealed to us. We love to tell the story of how God delivered Daniel from the lions.

It's a wonderful story, and, even better, it's true. But what shall we make of the fact that thousands of Christians were thrown to the lions in Rome and no angel appeared to deliver them?

We remember the three Hebrews thrown into a fire. Behold, one like unto the Son of Man walks with them! Indeed, when the three emerge, there is not even the smell of smoke on them. But where was the Son of Man when John Huss and other martyrs died in the flames?

There are two classes of heroes named in Hebrews 11. The author lists all those who triumphed over their enemies: Gideon, Barak, Samson, David, to name a few. Then we read abruptly, "And others experienced mockings and scourgings, yes, also chains and imprisonment. They were stoned, they were sawn in two, they were tempted, they were put to death" (vv. 36-37). Some were delivered, some were not; but both groups are heroes of faith.

This contrast is seen clearly in Acts 12. Herod kills James, the half-brother of Christ, with the sword. He intends to do the same to Peter, but the church prays for his deliverance, and he is miraculously released. One may try to explain Peter's release, saying that the church prayed for him and not for James. However, they did not even pray in faith for Peter; when the servant girl said that he was at the door, they assumed she was temporarily insane.

The effective, fervent prayer of a righteous man does accomplish much. It is the means God uses to fulfill His specific will. God wanted Daniel, the three Hebrews, and Peter delivered, and prayers offered in harmony with His purposes were answered.

What if God's people had not prayed in these cases? We cannot know whether these men would have been delivered or not. God often carries out His will with or without our intercession. We are sure, however, that these prayers would have been of benefit to those who prayed them, even if they had not been answered. The purpose of prayer is not so much to change God's mind about a particular circumstance as it is to change our hearts so that we accept whatever circumstances He gives us. As someone has said, it is much more important that we lay hold of God than that we lay hold of the answer we seek.

The idea that a prayer is useless unless it is answered is false. Many men and women of God have besought God for matters that did not come to pass, but they received much spiritual benefit, and God was honored. Prayer—even unanswered prayer—

enables us to develop intimacy with the Almighty. Getting an affirmative answer is not the only purpose of prayer.

In the final analysis we must submit our prayers to the inscrutable will of God, who has the right to do as He wishes with those who are His own. He has every right to treat each person differently.

THE PRIORITY OF GOD

Yet some questions still remain. Why all this unpredictability? Why this apparent divine disinterest in our plight? Why did the family of James have to suffer whereas the family of Peter experienced deliverance? Why are children of God not automatically protected from rape, accidents, and painful illnesses? If He wanted to, God could easily be more consistent and helpful.

Much is hidden in the counsels of God, but what God desires from us, despite His apparently haphazard dealings with us, is *faith*.

Think this through: if faith is God's ultimate priority for us, what better way could He test it than by refusing to answer a prayer to which we think He should say yes?

In order to illustrate the demands of faith, Basil Mitchell tells this parable:

In time of war in an occupied country, a member of the resistance meets with a stranger one night who deeply impresses him. They spend the night together in conversation. The stranger affirms that he also is on the side of the resistance—indeed he is in charge of it. He urges the young partisan to have faith in him—no matter what.

The young man is impressed with the stranger and decides to put his trust in him.

The next day he sees the stranger fight on the side of the resistance and he says to his friends, "The stranger is on our side." His faith is vindicated.

However, the following day the stranger is in the uniform of a policeman handing patriots to the occupying power—to the enemy!

The young man's friends murmur against him, insisting that the stranger could not be on their side. But the young partisan is undeterred, believing in the stranger no matter what.

Sometimes he asks for help from the stranger and receives it; sometimes he does not receive it. At times like this he affirms, "The stranger knows best."

This ambiguous behavior on the part of the stranger causes the young man's friends to ridicule his faith saying, "If that's what you mean by being on our side, the sooner he goes over to the other side the better!" Now the young man faces a dilemma: does he conclude that the stranger is not on his side after all, or does he go on believing no matter what?[3]

God has assured us in His Word that He is for us and that nothing shall separate us from His love. Yet His actions are ambiguous, sometimes seeming as if He is not on our side at all. What do we do? At what point can we say, "He does not care"?

The explanation is that it depends on the extent of our friendship with the Stranger (God). The better we know Him, the more likely it is that we will keep trusting Him, even when it appears that He is no longer on our side. We will not judge His love for us by circumstances but by His promises.

This is "the trial of our faith." God sees how much we are able to endure, while we continue to believe that He knows best. God chooses to do the opposite of what seems sensible to us. What a test of our loyalty!

Let's return to the young preacher from the beginning of this booklet. Suppose God wanted to create a set of circumstances that would stretch people's faith in His goodness and loving concern. How could He best do that, except by making it look as if He is acting in a way that belies those exact attributes? When He appears to be on the side of the enemy, do we still believe that He knows best? The question is, Can we believe Him, *no matter what?*

Now we are back to the question posed earlier: Does our heavenly Father really love us more than an earthly father, who is more immediately responsive to our needs and requests?

The answer is that our heavenly Father does love us more than our earthly father does, but He has a different set of priorities. We value health, and so does our heavenly Father. But He values faith even more. We value food, and so does our heavenly Father. But He values patience even more.

What God seeks to do within us is much more important to Him than what happens outside of us. Our circumstances are important to Him—the very hairs on our head are numbered. But more important, He seeks a devoted heart.

After John the Baptist was thrown into prison, he began to have second thoughts as to whether or not Christ was the Messiah. For one thing, the Old Testament predicted that when the Messiah came, the prisoners would be freed (Isaiah 61:1). John made the same error as those who believe that God is obligated to heal us: he misinterpreted the timing and application of that promise.

As John sat in the dungeon, it seemed that Christ was reneging on that promise in Isaiah. And wasn't it unfair that a man who had played such a vital part in Christ's early ministry should be so summarily set aside for taking a righteous stand against Herod's new marriage? So John sent a delegation to pointedly ask, "Are You the Expected One, or shall we look for someone else?" (Matthew 11:3).

In response, Jesus reminded John that miracles were being done and then added, "Blessed is he who keeps from stumbling over Me" (v. 6). We could paraphrase those words to say, "Blessed is the person who is not upset with the way I run my business."

Blessed is the person who does not say, "I'm never going to bother God with another request again."

Blessed is the person who understands that the purpose of prayer is not merely to get the things we want but to learn to accept whatever God gives us.

Blessed is the person who lets God be God.

Blessed is the person who believes God, no matter what.

Notes

1. Philip Yancey, *Where Is God When It Hurts* (Grand Rapids: Zondervan, 1977), p. 151.
2. "Here's Joni!" *Today's Christian Woman*, January/February 1990, pp. 24-25.
3. Basil Mitchell in *New Essays in Philosophical Theology*, eds. Anthony Flew and Alastair McIntyre (New York: Macmillan, 1955), pp. 103-4.